LEWD
LIMERICKS

LEWD
LIMERICKS

MICHAEL HORGAN

foulsham
LONDON • NEW YORK • TORONTO • SYDNEY

foulsham

The Publishing House, Bennetts Close, Cippenham, Slough, Berkshire, SL1 5AP, England

ISBN 0-572-02941-1

Printed in Great Britain by Cox & Wyman Ltd, Reading, Berkshire

Introduction

Firstly, a warning to the unwary:

Some verses contained in this book
Include four-letter words, such as 'fuck'.
They're rude and they're lewd,
They're not for the prude,
And if that upsets you – don't look!

If, on the contrary, you would describe yourself as
broad-minded with a keen sense of humour, then please read
on; for in the following pages you will find a selection of
original, unexpurgated and rib-tickling limericks which you
will want to share with like-minded friends and colleagues.

There can be little doubt that the limerick is the most popular
and original of English verse forms. Almost everyone, when
asked, can recite at least one favourite limerick, though he
may be hard-pressed to remember just a couple of lines of
'proper' poetry.

But what is it that makes the limerick so memorable? Perhaps
it is the quirky metre, or the deceptively simple structure, or
the economy of words – for in this case brevity is indeed the
soul of wit. Or has it to do primarily with the subject matter,
which usually ranges from the risqué through varying shades
of blue to the downright filthy? The answer probably lies in a
subtle combination of all these things. Many of the best and

most memorable of modern limericks are essentially dirty jokes cleverly dressed in verse – and given a certain intellectual legitimacy in the process.

Whatever the explanation, I hope you will discover within my new collection of limericks some that you will wish to add to your list of all-time personal favourites.

MICHAEL HORGAN

I'm a rhymer
Not a poet,
Just a rhymer
And I know it.

A large part of this type of verse
About practices lewd and perverse
    Is quite scatological
    Gynaecological
Bullshit. And some is much worse.

She's had hundreds of lovers, has Jenny,
She just can't remember how many,
    But of fellows like Jules,
    Who was born with two tools,
I doubt that she's had hardly any.

I once thought I loved you, monsieur,
But after tonight I'm not sure:
  You've gone off half-cock
  All over my frock
And left a big stain on the floor.

There was a young fellow from France
Whose tool was as sharp as a lance.
  No wonder the ladies
  Would always evade his
Polite invitations to dance.

When he woke with a pain in his head
And found someone else in his bed
    With her legs open wide,
    It wasn't his bride,
But her toothless old mother instead.

Since Pat has got married to Pete
Their happiness should be complete,
    But he's not been right
    Since their honeymoon night,
Which they spent in the Nutcracker Suite.

I know a young lady called Frances
Who makes a real hit when she dances.
    You should hear the lads shout
    While she waltzes about,
Revealing an absence of pantses.

There was a young lady from Buckingham
Whose pants were so tight she got
               stuck in 'em,
    So she called the police
    To assist her release,
And the last thing I heard she was
               filing a complaint.

When Julie was shagged by big Joel
With his muscular, seven-inch pole,
    She cried, 'Ow, that's sore,
    Are you perfectly sure
That you're shoving it up the right hole?'

My dear, you look simply divine,
And I know that we'll get along fine,
    For making ends meet
    Will be such a treat
When one end is yours, and one mine.

A foolish young streaker called Pete
Once ran in the nude down the street,
But the frosts of December
Perished his member
And rendered his manner effete.

When we went to a bistro in Cannes,
That's me and my girlfriend Joanne,
The *garçon*, the swine,
Dipped his prick in the wine
And offered Joanne *coq-au-vin*.

When a girl on an island remote
Met a Frenchman who lived in a boat,
    She was soon in his bunk
    With a mouth full of spunk
And a ruddy great Frog in her throat.

Well, this is my first real affair
And I'm dying to let down my hair,
    But I haven't a clue
    About just what to do –
So tell me, dear, what goes in where?

I'm in love, metaphorically speaking,
With a cute little lady from Peking,
    And intend to up-end her
    And give her pudenda
The sort of attention they're seeking.

I know that you're probably right
That Nelly is not very bright,
    But when we start screwing
    She knows what she's doing
And we screw several times every night.

Although he may seem quite a shy man
Please don't be fooled by young Simon:
    His tongue is so long
    And so supple and strong
That he used it to rupture my hymen.

Fitzpatrick, Fitzgerald and me
Are terribly gay company:
    FitzP fits FitzG
    And FitzG fits FitzP,
And each of those Fitzes fits me!

That noble hussar, Captain Kossoff,
Gave each of the troops he was boss of
    A buxom young wench
    For beating the French
And a pretty young boy for a toss off.

A clever young lady called Lu
Found a chimney sweep stuck up the flue,
    So seizing her chance
    She pulled down his pants
And relieved what had caused his to-do.

Though pandas do not like to screw
And a panda's orgasms are few,
    The vet makes them come
    Using fingers and thumb
And sprays the whole zoo with their goo.

My new secretary, Miss Pymme,
Seems frightfully proper and prim,
    And only I know
    How she lets herself go
If you stuff twenty quid up her quim.

At ninety, my Great Uncle Fred
Took a sexy young stripper to bed.
    I'm afraid I can't say
    If he had it away
'Cos it's wrong to speak ill of the dead.

I'm in love with a lady called Laura
And I'd do almost anything for her.
    It thrills her to bits
    When I nibble her tits
And grease her vagina with ... margarine.

A nimble young lady called Flo
Once diddled herself with her toe,
    But she now rues the day
    And she's too shy to say
Where her bunions have started to grow.

The usherettes down at the Forum
Are famed for their lack of decorum:
    You should see what they're willing
    To do for a shilling –
No wonder the guys all adore 'em.

I thought she'd be naughty but nice,
And she proved to be cheap at the price,
    With big hairy legs
    And teats like fried eggs
And a twat that was tight as a vice.

Pray tell me, dear, who is that chump,
Who stands there, all naked and plump,
    With his tool in his ear,
    Appearing from here
Like a rather obscene petrol pump?

A randy young cowboy from Dallas
Had little effect on Aunt Alice.
She said, 'I'm impressed,
But I wish you'd get dressed,
For there's more to a man than his phallus.'

Well, I'm glad that they didn't ask me
To that orgy at Flat 23.
It's okay for some
But for guys that can't come
An orgy is no place to be.

To make Father's Christmas Eve cheerier
Our Reverend Mother Superior
    Wears transparent scanties
    And open-crotch panties
And tinsel around her posterior.

Before Betty tempts you to sin, it
Is wise to reflect for a minute:
    By a quirk of design her
    Enormous vagina
Has several piranha fish in it.

I met a young thing from John's Wood,
Who said, 'If you feel in the mood,
 Unbutton my front
 And I'll show you my ...' can't
Tell you the rest, 'cos it's rude.

One glance at our new Chief of Staff
Is enough to make anyone laugh.
 The silly old fool
 Has a seven-foot tool,
Which he drapes round his neck like a scarf.

The Chief of Police in Algiers
Is not the nice man he appears:
    He gets great delight out of
    Kicking the shite out of
Paedophiles, harlots and queers.

I agree that, on closer inspection,
You achieve a prodigious erection,
    Yet I have to protest
    That to see you undressed
Still fills me with no great affection.

Sister Josephine stripped off her habit
And made frantic love to the abbot,
Then, pausing for breath,
Cried, 'A fate worse than death,
Is to die without once having had it!'

How sad to see someone like Yates
In such impecunious straits:
The reason, of course, is
Fast women, slow horses
And the sailors he frequently dates.

They say that our parson's young daughter
Loved sex like no decent girl oughter,
But nothing she did
Stimulated her id
Like the spanking she got when he caught her.

How easily Ernie arouses
The passions of other men's spouses.
It seems that the reason
They find him so pleasin'
Is that thing sticking out of his trousers.

The reverend vicar of Bude
When sleep-walking totally nude,
　　Arrived quite by chance
　　At a charity dance
And tossed off all over the food.

A silly young woman called Sue
Has sealed up her fanny with glue.
　　This stops her, she says,
　　Having casual lays,
Which is vexing but probably true.

I know a young woman called Frances,
Who often strips off when she dances,
    And the more she reveals,
    The surer one feels
That her name should be Francis, not Frances.

There's a lecherous lady who claims
That, while having it off with young James,
    The fires of desire
    Burned higher and higher
Till his teddy bear burst into flames.

A horny old lecher named Fletcher
Was also an amateur sketcher
        Of girls in the nude,
        Who he usually screwed,
And did they enjoy it? You betcha!

There was a young fellow from Tonga
Whose donger grew longer and longer,
        So he had it away
        In a rather strange way
With a short-sighted, seven-foot conger.

While she lies on her back, legs asunder,
Her crack is an object of wonder.
    She shows it to me,
    Being Aussie, you see,
'Cos she knows that I like it down under.

The wang of the orang-utan
Way down by its ankles doth hang,
    But stands three foot eight
    In its tumescent state –
No wonder it loves a good bang!

When God made his prototype man
He lost vital parts of the plan
    And unsightly sections
    Like bums and erections
He ought to improve when he can.

They say that the good King Canute
Was wont to get pissed as a newt
    And wander about
    With his prick sticking out,
Whilst playing lewd songs on his lute.

A sturdy young fellow in Poole
Was blessed with a marvellous tool.
    When fully extended
    The bloody thing ended
A couple of miles north of Goole.

A marriage needs more than mere lust,
It needs friendship, affection and trust;
    But I'd like to suggest
    That we both get undressed
And make sure we're compatible first.

A young public schoolboy each day
Would go down on his knees and thus pray:
    'Oh Lord, if you can,
    Please make me a man,
And Lord, please make sure that he's gay.'

The lusty young lads of Lismore
Have tools of eight inches or more,
    But ladies, be calm,
    There's no cause for alarm –
They haven't a clue what they're for.

Have all the girls other than me got
A place in their cunts called the G spot?
    I've tried with vibrators
    And big sweet potatoes
But so far I haven't found *the* spot.

I met a young girl from Havana,
Who was known for her down-to-earth manner.
    She said: 'Beg your pardon,
    But is that a hard on,
And if not, would you pass a banana?'

An Australian girl in Earl's Court
Did things that no decent girl ought:
    Her talents fellatic
    Made men quite ecstatic —
Back home she'd be called a real sport!

There was a young girl from Dundrum,
Who swore she would never succumb,
    But she did, in the end,
    With a friend of a friend,
Who helped her to come with his thumb.

'My brain,' said this girl from Athlone,
'Is my major erogenous zone.'
    Quite a clever idea
    But the reason, I fear,
Why she spends so much time on her own.

Concerning the question of cunts,
You really must see Helen Hunt's,
    With carrots and candles
    And hockey stick handles
She does some remarkable stunts.

Well, here we both are in the hay
And I'm dying to have a good lay,
    For a red-blooded male
    Likes a nice bit of tail —
But this one has fur and says 'Neigh'!

I know a young girl called Virginia,
Whose figure is basically linear.
    Her vital statistics
    Resemble a dipstick's,
In fact, she just couldn't be skinnier.

There was a young fellow from Harrow
Whose prick was as big as a marrow
    And, needless to say,
    It got in his way,
So he carted it round in a barrow.

The Campbells, the couple next door,
Are over-sexed people, I'm sure,
    And it sounds by the shrieks
    And the way their bed creaks
That the Campbells are coming once more.

Our dentist, well known for his suavity,
Committed a sin of some gravity:
　　First he undressed his nurse,
　　Then, to make matters worse,
He set about filling her cavity.

A foolish old codger from Goring
Was asked why he'd taken up whoring.
　　'It's simple,' he said,
　　'My wife is stone dead,
And necrophilia's simply dead boring.'

A clumsy young fellow called Natrass
Once jumped into bed with an actress,
But missed her completely
And drilled, rather neatly,
A ruddy great hole in her mattress.

I must say I got a bit flustered,
When Tom stuck his tool in the custard
And grumpily said:
'You won't come to bed,
So I'm sitting here, fucking disgusted.'

There once was a hoary old Boer,
Who had it away with a whoer,
    Once in the stable
    And twice on the table
And three times or moer on the floer.

A horny young butcher called Marcus
Was found in the freezer quite starkers,
    His prick turning blue
    While attempting to screw
The rear of a freshly hung carcass.

Whenever I've nothing to do,
I jerk myself off — well, don't you?
    In fact, I'm so slick
    At jerking my dick
That I've no inclination to screw!

Sir Walter the Spanish engages,
Forsaking his lady for ages,
    So she goes to bed
    With a good book instead,
And often a couple of pages.

They say that in Paris the whores
Prefer to be fucked on all fours,
    And for the same price,
    If you treat them real nice,
They perform lots of clever encores.

I'm in love with a young female copper,
Who loves to be screwed good and proper,
    Which is all very fine,
    But we screw all the time
And I've blisters all over my chopper.

Samantha is leaving to brighten
The lives of the people in Huyton;
All the boys that she knows
Will be sad when she goes –
When she comes it is really excitin'.

An addled old fellow called Heath
Once bought from the chemist a sheath,
Then attempted to screw
A stripper called Sue –
So who wants to lay the next wreath?

I know a young man in Calcutta,
Who plasters his member with butter,
    Then lovingly screws
    A sack of cashews –
He must be a real fucking nutter!

I once knew a fellow called Scotty,
Whose habits were awfully grotty:
    In five minutes flat
    He had buggered my cat
And tossed himself off in my potty.

A woman who lived in Bermuda
Surprised a nocturnal intruder.
　　To make him feel randy
　　She poured him a brandy
And tickled his balls while he screwed her.

A dusky young maiden from Goa
Invited me upstairs to show her
　　A kinky position
　　For having coition,
Then gave me a tenner to blow her.

I wish I knew more about Jim's
Unusual sexual whims,
　　Many of which
　　Involve pneumatic tits
And synthetic, customised quims.

Last Saturday Sue came to call:
She really has no shame at all.
　　She said, 'Though I like
　　To come on my bike,
I come on your cock best of all.'

A sexually naive young sailor,
Concerned about being a failure,
  Was screwed every day
  In the nautical way
By the crew of a Japanese whaler.

I must say the chaps were impressed
When Valerie took off her vest
  In that nonchalant way
  And asked them to play
With the two great big lumps on her chest.

A circus performer called Nick
Has mastered a marvellous trick:
    With consummate ease
    He can swing through the trees
With the aid of his prehensile prick.

A native who lived by the Nile
Had sex with a big crocodile,
    But when he was in her
    She had him for dinner,
Which accounts for the crocodile's smile.

When Martin screwed Maud on his pillion,
He said to her, 'Maud, thanks a million,
    I love a tight twat
    But yours beats the lot
And my penis is turning vermilion!'

'The trouble with mermaids,' said Herman,
That miserable, sex-starved young merman,
    'Is not that their tails
    Are covered with scales,
It's the lack of a crack to shoot sperm in!'

A vulgar young fellow called Janus
Could fart the *Last Post* through his anus.
    He may think it's smart
    And call it an art,
But I think young Janus is heinous.

No wonder the French mistress hates
That randy young bugger called Bates.
    He just has to catch
    A whiff of her snatch
And young Master Bates masturbates.

A rather strange chap is young Danny:
He's fallen in love with his nanny,
      And keeps in his pocket
      A little gold locket
Containing some hairs from her fanny.

When first we made love, you and me,
You were randy as randy could be,
      And your cute little cunny
      Produced so much honey
That we had some left over for tea.

A silly old farmer from Wendover
Told his busty young milkmaid to bend over,
 Then he planted his tool,
 Till his wife said, 'You fool,
You're shoving it up the wrong end of her.'

Young Stephen is such a seducer,
He can take any girl and reduce her
 To begging for more
 As she writhes on the floor,
And he's too well brought up to refuse her.

My grandma, who seldom was ill,
Left this useful advice in her will:
    'A lay every day
    Keeps the doctor away,
As long as you're taking the pill.'

Though parting can be such a shame,
Their marriage has not been the same,
    Since she found him sunk
    To his bollocks in spunk
Up the arse of the pantomime dame.

Whenever you're anxious to score,
Just say to your girl, *'Je t'adore.'*
    With charm you will win her
    And once you are in her
You'll soon have her squealing *'Encore!'*

I once knew a girl called Annetta,
Who bought an enormous red setter,
    Which licked her left tit,
    Then nuzzled her slit
Till she couldn't say stop. Then it ate her.

Our teacher of French said to Pam,
'It is clear that you don't give a damn.'
　　So she undid his flies
　　With a gleam in her eyes,
And she soon passed her oral exam.

When Angus was kicked out of Troon
For farting too loud out of tune,
　　The big ignoramus
　　Plugged up his anus
And now he's a weather balloon.

Now Brenda is married to Dan
She thinks he's a marvellous man:
    Midst nappies and dishes,
    Whenever she wishes,
He fucks her with verve and elan.

That winsome young chap from Assisi
Is not very masculine, is he?
    He sits down to piss
    Like a regular miss –
No wonder they call him a cissy.

I really don't think our stenographers
Should pose in the nude for photographers.
　　These shots of pudenda
　　Will only engender
The interest of back-street pornographers.

There was a fine fellow called Avery,
Whose spunk was uncommonly savoury.
　　His missus, of course,
　　Found it cheaper than sauce,
And it made all her stews taste more flavoury.

Said a learned professor called Pluck:
'Look, I've read every erudite book
        By Descartes and Kant,
        But what I most want
Is a wild Rabelaisian fuck!'

A maiden from Juan-les-Pins
Would pray every night for a man
        To roger her twat
        With his big you-know-what
(Because 'prick' doesn't properly scan).

No wonder young women would cower
On meeting bold Owen Glendower,
 They say he had balls
 Like the dome of St Paul's
And a prick like the Post Office Tower.

Our teacher of maths is a Scot,
But tight she is certainly not.
 In fact, we deduce,
 That by regular use,
We have doubled the size of her twat.

I know a young lady from Tring,
Who certainly knows how to swing,
  She performs pagan rites
  In open-crotch tights
With a daffodil stuck up her thing,

The usherette down at the Ritz
Has a marvellous pair of big tits,
  Which she keeps nice and firm
  By massaging with sperm
Whenever her boyfriend permits.

The women round here are extreme
In matters of oral hygiene:
    They never fellate
    The guys that they date
Unless they squirt pasteurised cream.

If your life has become rather stale,
What you need is a red-blooded male,
    Who is thoughtful, refined,
    Romantic and kind,
And will come twice a night without fail.

When it comes to the matter of love,
It is Eric I'm envious of;
  He was born with five pricks,
  So he pulls all the chicks
And his underpants fit like a glove.

My girlfriend is only a wee thing
But with lust she is constantly seething:
  When I bought a vibrator
  To try to placate her,
The bloody thing knocked her front teeth in.

A rather gay actor called Fox
Was often found down in the docks
    In his favourite role,
    Which was filling his hole
With big, burly stevedores' cocks.

There once was an ugly old hag
Who was dying to have a good shag,
    So she lay in the street
    With her pants at her feet
And her head in a brown paper bag.

That popular man-about-town
And lover of curry, called Brown,
  Farts natural gas
  Through a pipe up his ass,
Thus keeping his heating bills down.

There once was an African queen,
Whose feasts were a sight to be seen,
  And what she liked most
  Were bollocks on toast —
Her eunuchs, of course, were less keen.

At first she declared that she wouldn't,
Then later she whispered she shouldn't,
    But when she gave in
    After two pints of gin
She lay down and found that she couldn't!

Since Teddy was told that he oughter
Stop drinking his favourite porter,
    His regular tipple
    Comes straight from the nipple
Of Laura, the landlady's daughter.

A randy but short-sighted thief
Attempted to rape Mrs Heath,
So he leapt on her bed,
But he missed, and instead,
He buggered her butler beneath.

The prick of the vicar of Fife
Is the longest I've seen in my life.
He stands in the garden
And uses his hard on
To prop up the clothes for his wife.

Beware of young Septimus Sands,
He's the guy with the wandering hands,
    Which are frequently found
    Groping around
Convenient mammary glands.

I once laid a lady from Leek,
Whose sexual responses were weak:
    At the height of orgasm
    She gave one small spasm
And a barely perceptible squeak.

Young virgins, whatever they do,
Should never say 'How' to a Sioux:
    A Sioux needs no urging
    To show a young virgin
How Sioux you-know-what, i.e., screw.

Look, Doctor, I don't think it's funny
To be told, when I've spent so much money,
    That your diagnosis
    Is myxomatosis
From having it off with a bunny!

At the age of one hundred and four
My Pa died in bed with a whore,
Who said, 'It's a shame
That he went when he came,
But he went with a bang, that's for sure!'

When the Good Lord created my Dinah,
He didn't take care to design her
The way that he should have
Or he never would have
Left sandpaper up her vagina.

I'm in love with a lady called Lyn,
And sex is her favourite sin:
　　She wriggles, she sighs,
　　She opens her thighs,
Then she gives me a vertical grin.

It's terribly hard to resist
Having my John Thomas kissed,
　　But nothing you do
　　Will be much use to you
When its owner is so Brahms and Liszt.

'Twas the Caliph of Baghdad's proud boast
That he was the world's finest host,
But, as for his harem,
He nightly would scare 'em
By serving fresh penis pot roast.

Gipsy Rose Lee, wife of Sid,
Was famed for the dances she did:
As everyone knows,
She wore very few clothes,
And she'd show you her quim for a quid.

Said Malcolm McTavish from Bute,
As he buggered a male prostitute:
    'Well, the love of my life
    Has run off with my wife,
So one has to find some substitute.'

I know a male stripper called Noel,
Who is blessed with a thirteen-inch pole,
    And he's doing all right
    Giving three shows a night —
Well, it's better than life on the dole.

A barmaid in fair Enniskillen
Will do you-know-what for a shilling:
    A case, so to speak,
    Of a spirit that's weak
And flesh that is certainly willing.

A certain romantic young poet
Put dung on his donger to grow it,
    So people would talk
    Of the length of his stalk
And the size of the bollocks below it.

A lively young lass from Blantyre
Succumbed to her lover's desire
  And, when he was in,
  Jabbed his arse with a pin,
Which made him go in even higher.

Her daddy has carefully taught her
To be an obedient daughter,
  She gives all she's got
  For a dollar a shot
And she'll tickle your balls for a quarter.

She climbed off her lover and said:
'Well, we've bust every spring in the bed,
     And as you can see
     We have wrecked the settee,
So let's do it standing instead.'

When I went for a roll in the clover
With a frisky young maiden from Dover,
     We lay midst the flowers
     And made love for hours,
Till her dad, who's an umpire, called 'Over!'

Farmer Giles ain't as daft as he seems,
As he stands there and foolishly beams,
    'Cos under his smock,
    Caressing his cock,
Is Gertrude, the girl of his dreams.

When we went to the beach in the nude,
A terrible problem ensued:
    The sight of my prick
    Made my wife feel quite sick,
And it's nearly a year since we've screwed.

Sue has spent so much time in the sack,
Taking big hairy cocks up her crack,
    With macho young men
    Coming time and again,
That she's slipped every disc in her back.

Old Tom was the talk of Nantucket,
If anything moved he would fuck it:
    He was up a girl guide
    On the night that he died –
A fine way of kicking the bucket!

When fielding at deep extra cover,
I was somewhat surprised to discover
    A naked young lass
    Stretched out on the grass,
While third man made love to her mother.

That cunning old codger called Custer
Would make the maid feel all a-fluster,
    For the lecherous flirt
    Would lift up her skirt
And tickle her quim with a duster.

A lusty young lass from Toledo
Encountered a wayward torpedo,
    Which she started to screw
    Then it went off and blew
A bloody great hole where she peed-o.

God bless the young women of Wales,
Who have been jolly good to us males:
    With amorous arts
    They tickle our parts
And their hearts are as warm as their tails.

It is said that Arabian sheikhs
Can make love without stopping for weeks,
And their wives, it appears,
Can keep coming for years –
It sounds like they're all fucking freaks!

A prudish young teacher from York
Has this very peculiar walk,
And it's sad to relate
What has caused her strange gait –
She has plugged her vagina with chalk!

What sends the girls arse over tits
About Angelo's banana splits,
    Is not that they're long,
    And shaped like his dong,
It's the taste of his cream on their lips.

Said Sam, as he buried his cue
In Sue's quim and proceeded to screw:
    'The girl of my dreams
    Isn't coming, it seems,
But you do make a good number two.'

When Fred started farting like thunder,
He got quite concerned, and no wonder,
    And he corked up his ass
    So the gas could not pass –
Then he blew his whole backside asunder!

A wayward young cleric from Leicester
Fell in love with a lady called Heicester.
    He kissed and carreicester,
    Undressed and posseicester,
And then, as an afterthought, bleicester.

A fortunate fellow called Sandon
Was born with a seven-inch stand on.
    The midwife said, 'God,
    How exceedingly odd!'
As he shagged her with carefree abandon.

There's nothing excites Mrs Hollick
Like a down-to-earth sexual frolic:
    She thinks 69
    Is especially fine,
Though she wakes the next morning with colic.

A bashful young fellow from Arden
Once boarded a bus with a hard on,
    And a woman near by
    Stuck her hand in his fly
Without even begging his pardon.

See it standing there, strong and defiant,
The dong of the Jolly Green Giant,
    Hear the merry maids shout
    As they jerk it about,
Pulling off cream by the piant.

My wife has this act as a stripper:
Each night, while I pull down my zipper,
     She takes off her drawers
     To tremendous applause
And rides up and down my big dipper.

Tim took out his stiffy to stuff it
Up the welcoming cunt of Miss Muffet
     But, try as he might,
     Her cunt was too tight,
So Tim only managed to muff it.

I once knew a kinky young lass,
Who loved to shove things up her ass:
 If you studied her crap
 You would find bits of scrap,
Such as ornaments made out of brass.

A lady of leisure called Hope
Once filled her vagina with soap,
 And the suds that ensued
 The next time she screwed
Practically drowned the old dope.

A newly-wed fellow from Bandon
Just couldn't achieve a firm stand on.
 His wife tried all night
 To get it upright,
For her motto was *'Nil Desperandum'*.

Oh sexy, salacious Miss Plum!
When I asked her which way she had come,
 She answered, 'By train.'
 I replied, 'Come again?'
And she did, with my prick up her bum.

There was a young man from Ostend,
Whose member could nearly extend
    All the way over
    From Ostend to Dover
With hardly a hint of a bend.

Herr Offenbach's lusty young frau
Is such a lascivious cow.
    The butcher and baker
    With candlesticks make her,
Though I'm not sure I understand how.

There was a young cowboy out West,
Whose prick reached right up to his chest.
    Girls fainted with fright
    At the terrible sight,
So he hid it away in his vest.

In Kenya there live chimpanzees,
Whose bollocks hang down to their knees,
    And their dongs are so long
    And so supple and strong,
They can use them to swing through the trees.

A certain Carthusian monk
Got *non-compos mentis* when drunk.
    He stripped off his habit,
    Then buggered the abbot
And covered his sandals with spunk.

Far away where the baobab grows
Lives a tribe of nomadic negroes,
    Less quick on their feet
    Than most natives you meet,
'Cos their bollocks hang down to their toes.

A gifted musician called Amos
In musical circles was famous,
    For it's novel, you know,
    To be able to blow
Such melodious tunes through one's anus.

A supple young lady called Kimberly
Found Santa Claus stuck in her chimberly.
    An eight-inch erection
    Had jammed his mid-section,
But she soon solved the problem quite nimberly.

A nasty old fellow called Mark
Would wander around after dark
    Getting his kicks
    Doing perverted tricks
With nude statuettes in the park.

We really must treat with more gravity
The numerous acts of depravity
    Of those two nasty queers
    Who've been at it for years
Called Ben Doone and Philip McCavity.

There was a fair maiden called Brenda,
An innocent girl, warm and tender,
 Until she got stewed
 And danced around nude,
Displaying her feminine gender.

Although Harvey's habits were coarse,
His wife didn't file for divorce
 Till she caught him one day
 As he had it away
With the rear of a pantomime horse.

The gamest young chick in Chicago,
A student of music called Margot,
    Is able to fart
    A sizeable part
Of the theme song from *Doctor Zhivago*.

Look, darling, I'm not blaming you
For this tampon I've found in the stew:
    The taste is okay
    But please take it away —
It is not very easy to chew!

A buxom young lady from Deal,
When asked if her huge boobs were real,
    Replied, 'If it please you
    To give them a squeeze, you
Can tell if they burst or I squeal!'

Have you heard of the lady from Cheam,
Whose breasts were a sight to be seen?
    The left was quite cute
    But the right was minute
And the one in the middle gave cream.

When Gwendoline went to Paree,
All she could say was, *'Oui, oui.'*
    She soon passed away
    From exposure, they say,
Having laid the whole *gendarmerie*.

I once knew a girl called Sophia,
Who really inflamed my desire
    By rubbing with Sloane's
    My erogenous zones,
Which just about set them on fire.

That fat girl who works in accounts
Is one of my favourite mounts.
    It's rather like humping
    An over-ripe pumpkin –
All squelchy and soft where it counts.

I'm in love with a fellow called Frank
With a cock like the gun on a tank,
    And there's nothing so grand
    As to take him in hand
And give him a jolly good wank.

The ladies of Shoeburyness
Will have sex only under duress:
　　They have an aversion
　　To any diversion
That leaves all their clothes in a mess.

When Jane wore her black leotard
My pecker grew horny and hard,
　　So we had it away
　　Without further delay
And there wasn't a single hole barred.

On meeting a good-looking Wren,
A sex-starved young sailor called Ken
    Came straight to attention
    And, needless to mention,
He shafted her daft there and then.

A pretty young waitress called Glenda,
Was a flower of the feminine gender,
    Till one day, by mistake,
    She made cherry milkshake
By catching her tits in the blender.

I know a game girl called Anita,
Who drinks home-made wine by the litre.
    It's cheaper than whisky
    And makes her more frisky,
So you'll have a good time when you meet her.

We're getting quite peeved about Norma's
Obsession with handsome sixth-formers.
    She thrills them to bits
    Doing cartwheels and splits
Wearing nothing but purple leg warmers.

Whenever he meets pretty birds,
Our vicar, who's one of life's turds,
     Commences undressing them,
     Instead of blessing them,
For actions speak louder than words.

They say that the noble Sir Lancelot
With wayward young women would dance a lot,
     While they, in their fashion,
     Would kindle his passion,
So Lancelot came in his pants a lot.

Of lovers I've had quite a few
But none of them thrilled me like you,
   Your fabulous twat
   Is so juicy and hot
That it drives me quite wild when we screw.

So let's raise our glasses to Pat,
Who has managed, in ten minutes flat,
   To suck off the semen
   Of five able seamen,
The mate and the admiral's cat.

I'm in love with a jolly Jewess,
But she's sexually almost u.s.,
    We last had a screw
    Back in '72 —
And then she refused to undress.

My grandmother frequently falls
For young men in billiard halls.
    She loves their deep screws
    And the length of their cues
And the regular kissing of balls.

The captain loves Rose to repose
In his bunk with his prick twixt her toes,
    And to slowly fellate
    The horny first mate,
While the midshipman cries, 'There she blows!'

I know a young girl from Dundalk,
Who has plugged up her quim with a cork.
    Her motives aren't moral,
    She still has sex oral,
But she's terribly scared of the stork.

My buddy called Jack from Fort Knox
Is well hung and strong as an ox.
 My big sister Gwen
 Likes her men to be men,
So she often has Jack in her box.

Well, you may be a famous MP
But you're not all you're cracked up to be:
 I just can't remember
 When your standing member
Last lost its deposit in me.

A nasty young man from Japan
Attempted to rape Marianne,
    But the end of his gender
    Snapped her suspender
Which shot off his balls with a twang.

We've got a new cook from Genoa
And it's worthwhile you getting to know her,
    'Cos the scabs from her crack
    Make a really nice snack
When garnished with spermatozoa.

A shepherd, who had a prize flock,
Believed it might improve the stock
    If he rogered each one,
    So he started at dawn,
But by noon he had ruptured his cock.

※※※※※※※※※

'You bastard!' cried Kathy to Keith,
'Your fickleness beggars belief.
    It's easy to see
    You've been cheating on me
By the curly black hairs in your teeth!'

'My darling,' she said with a smile,
'I must say you fuck with great style,
    But three times a minute
    Is over the limit —
Do you mind if we rest for a while?'

It isn't much fun smoking pot
And I'm bored with my luxury yacht.
    No, my favourite toy
    Is the prick on that boy,
And I play with it rather a lot.

A rather odd Scotsman called Jock
Insists upon wearing a frock,
     Though the cold winter breezes
     That blow round his kneeses
Have frozen the end of his sporran.

That pretty young model called Clare
Has a beautiful mane of blonde hair
     But everyone knows,
     When she takes off her clothes,
That she's really a brunette down there.

The first time he started to shag her,
The wife of a fellow called Jagger
    Shouted, 'Hell's teeth,
     Please put on a sheath –
Your dick is as sharp as a dagger!'

There once was a frightful old hussy,
Who wasn't the slightest bit fussy
    About how many men
     Stuck what, where or when,
Up her poxy promiscuous pussy.

There once was a coolie called Wong,
Whose dong was incredibly long.
It may sound absurd,
But last night I heard
He was fucking the arse off King Kong.

I met a young woman called Dawn,
Who had a real penchant for porn.
When we went on a date
She just couldn't wait
For a chance to start blowing my horn.

No wonder my pecker gets rigid,
Whenever I'm in bed with Brigid:
    She tries every trick
    To pleasure my dick
To prove that she's really not frigid.

I know a young lady called Pat,
Who is really prodigiously fat,
    Like a great tub of lard,
    And it's terribly hard
To find the way into her twat.

Her ladyship said to McDuff,
As he shot his load into her muff:
      'Oh dear, not again,
       One shouldn't complain,
But five times a night is enough.'

We lay side by side on the grass,
That's me and this ex-convent lass,
      When a wandering mole
      In search of a hole
Got stuck up her tight little ass.

That over-sexed dingbat called Danny
Just cannot resist a hot fanny:
 This morning he took
 One look at the cook
And filled every nook in her cranny.

I'm dying to meet Shirley Knott,
The girl with the generous twat,
 Which could take, in its prime,
 Several tools at a time —
But the Pontypool pack? Surely not!

A rather strange lass called Tess Tickle
Would frequently cut off and pickle
    Bits of her lovers
    Such as me, amongst others,
Which is why I have only one testicle.

I must say I got quite a shock,
When I opened the door to your knock,
    And there you were standing
    Quite nude on the landing
With lipstick all over your cock.

The girls in the bistro allege,
That the cocky new waiter called Reg,
  When asked to display
  The Dish of the Day,
Showed them his meat and two veg.

A second-row forward that I know
Is built like an African rhino:
  He's big and he's brawny,
  He's hard and he's horny,
And his foreskin's as tough as old lino.

The last time I had a blind date,
I must say it wasn't that great.
    To tell you the truth
    It was rather uncouth
The way that he buggered my mate.

A sexy young lady called Gail
Had a permanent itch in her tail.
    When the weather was bad,
    She frequently had
Any good sport in a gale.

There's really no doubting that Joanie's
Most active erogenous zone is
    Her cute little muff,
    'Cos she can't get enough
Of bouncing about on fat ponies.

I can see why my kid brother Billy
Is driving his new girlfriend silly:
    The randy rapscallion
    Is hung like a stallion
And she has a cunt like a filly.

I've got a new lover called Amos,
Whose exploits in bed are quite famous,
    And I don't mind a bit
    When he diddles my slit,
But I won't take his cock up my anus.

The girls on the island of Herm
Have tits that are lovely and firm,
    But nothing's as fine as
    Their juicy vaginas
All dripping with freshly shot sperm.

Pam's partner is eager and young
With a beautiful butt, and well hung,
     But what makes her get
     All het up and wet
Is the dextrous use of his tongue.

Our teacher of sex education
Began with a live demonstration:
     While Fortescue Minor
     Licked her vagina,
The class practised mixed masturbation.

I love you a lot in my fashion,
And I'm really impressed with your passion
    When your muscular pole
    Is at work in my hole –
But five times a night is your ration.

In Queensland a farmer called Blue
Had sex with a wild kangaroo.
    It must be fun humping
    A roo when it's jumping –
I'd give it a go, wouldn't you?

I doubt if it's morally right,
And it certainly isn't polite,
    To photograph fannies
    Of elderly grannies
While they're sitting there having a shite.

There once was a cheeky young miss,
Who said to her boyfriend, called Chris,
    'When you've done with my tits,
    It would thrill me to bits,
If you turned your attention to this.'

I know a loose fellow called Leo,
Who spends every weekend in Rio,
    Where it's easy to find
    Young girls who don't mind
His sticking his prick where they pee-o.

A few minutes after I met her,
I said to my girlfriend, Rosetta,
    'A peck on the cheek
    Is hardly unique –
A peck on the pecker is better.'

When Dangerous Dan grabbed Belinda,
And to the four-poster he pinned her,
 The heat that ensued,
 As they screwed and they screwed,
Nearly burned his old man to a cinder.

Horrid things happened in Whittingham.
Though nobody there liked admitting 'em;
 Necrophilia was
 Abolished because
Some rotten old cunt went and split on 'em.

A kinky and avant-garde German,
Whose name, I remember, was Herman,
    Made films of the cunnies
    Of young Playboy bunnies
In close-up with lots of fresh sperm in.

When Barbara's boyfriend defied her
To drink a whole gallon of cider,
    She did, and passed out,
    But came to with a shout,
While her boyfriend was coming inside her.

A newly-wed fellow called Pickup
Found it difficult getting his dick up
    His bashful young bride,
    But he tried and he tried,
Till she came with a lady-like hiccup.

I once met a cute little nurse
Whose habits were rather perverse:
    She wore rubber knickers
    And solicited vicars
To have sex in the back of a hearse.

There's a humanoid up here on Venus
With a luminous, sixteen-inch penis,
    And all night he hunts
    For big hairy cunts –
Oh shit! Look out girls, he has seen us!

I said to my girlfriend called Heather,
'I won't go to church in such weather;
    There's much to be said
    For staying in bed
And playing our organs together.'